BIOMETRICS: FUNDAMENTAL

Dr. Snehlata Barde

Professor

MATS School of Information Technology

MATS University, Raipur, Chhattisgarh, INDIA

Copyright © 2022 by Snehlata Barde

All rights reserved. This book or any portion thereof may not be reproduced or used in any manner whatsoever without the express written permission of the publisher except for the use of brief quotations in a book review.

Imprint: Lulu.com

ISBN 978-1-6780-3182-4

ent
Biometrics: Fundamental

Preface

Digital image processing is a wide area of research biometrics is one of them. Biometrics is a technique that is used for the authentication of the biological features of a person. It is most useful for a person's identification and verification. There are several types of biometric security technologies based on the physiological and behavioral characteristics of the person are used. A lot of research contributions have been made by numerous researchers.

This book covers all major aspects of biometrics: Introduction to biometrics, Need and challenges in Biometrics; Biometrics physiological and behavioral modalities; Biometrics authentication system; Multimodal biometrics system; Fusion levels and techniques; some applications implementation of face recognition, ear recognition, iris recognition, foot recognition.

TABLE OF CONTENTS

CHAPTER-1 **INTRODUCTION**		**1-4**
1.1	Introduction to Biometrics	1
1.2	Need of Biometrics	2
1.3	Challenges in Biometrics	2
CHAPTER-2 **BIOMETRIC MODALITIES**		**5-13**
2.1	Physiological Traits	5
	2.1.1 Face biometrics	6
	2.1.2 Ear biometrics	7
	2.1.3 Fingerprint biometrics	7
	2.1.4 Footprint biometrics	8
	2.1.5 Hand Geometry biometrics	9
	2.1.6 Iris biometrics	10
2.2	Behavioral Traits	11
	2.3.1 Voice biometrics	11
	2.3.2 Signature biometrics	12

	2.3.3 Keystroke biometrics	12
CHAPTER-3	**BIOMETRIC AUTHENTICATION SYSTEM**	**14-18**
3.1	Enrolment Process	14
3.2	The training involved in Biometric System	15
3.3	Testing involved in Biometric System	17
CHAPTER-4	**MULTIMODAL BIOMETRICS SYSTEM**	**19-24**
4.1	Multimodal Biometrics	19
4.2	The architecture of Unimodal Biometrics System	21
4.3	The architecture of Multimodal Biometrics System	22
4.3	Drawbacks of Unimodal biometric System	23
CHAPTER-5	**FUSION LEVELS AND TECHNIQUES**	**25-36**
5.1	Introduction to Fusion levels	25
	5.1.1 Fusion Level Prior to matching	26
	5.1.2 Fusion Level After to matching	27

5.2	The Fusion Technique	31
5.3	Normalization Technique	35

CHAPTER-6 FACE RECOGNITION   37-42

6.1	Face Recognition	37
6.2	Principal Component Analysis	39

CHAPTER -7 EAR RECOGNITION   43-47

7.1	Ear Recognition	43
7.2	Eigen Image	44

CHAPTER-8 IRIS RECOGNITION   48-56

8.1	Iris Recognition	48
8.2	Segmentation	49
8.3	Normalization and Encoding	52
8.4	Iris Matching	55

CHAPTER-9 FOOT RECOGNITION   57-64

9.1	Foot Recognition	57
9.2	Sequential Modified Haar Wavelet Transform Method	59

CHAPTER-10   CONCLUSION   65

REFERENCES

List of Figure

1. Fig.2.1 Physiological traits of a person 10
2. Fig.2.2 Behavioural traits of a person.......13
3. Fig.3.1 Enrolment process...................15
4. Fig. 3.2 Training process involved in biometrics.......................................16
5. Fig. 3.3 Testing process involved in biometrics...................................17
6. Fig. 4.1 Multimodal Biometric system.....20
7. Fig.4.2 Architecture of Unimodal Biometrics System...21
8. Fig.4.3 Architecture of Multimodal Biometrics System...............................22
9. Fig. 5.1 Different Fusion Schemes..........30
10. Fig. 6.1 Face recognition process...........38
11. Fig. 6.2 Training set of faces................41
12. Fig. 6.3 Eigenfaces of facial images of the image database..............................42
13. Fig. 7.1 Anatomy of the ear 43
14. Fig. 7.2 Ear recognition system.............45

15. Fig. 7.3 Grayscale images of ears...........46
16. Fig. 7.4 Eigen images of ears 47
17. Fig. 8.1 Human eye highlighting iris and other parts 48
18. Fig. 8.2 The rubber sheet model.............52
19. Fig. 8.3 Cropped and grayscale image of eye..53
20. Fig. 8.4 Segmented iris region............ ..54
21. Fig. 9.1 Footprint biometric system........ 58
22. Fig. 9.2 Footprint identification system....60
23. Fig. 9.3 Cropped and grayscale image of foot...61
24. Fig. 9.4 Foot image in 4x4 blocks..........63

CHAPTER 1

INTRODUCTION

Biometrics is a common system used in various applications such as student/employee attendance, traffic and toll monitoring; identification and verification of a person, etc. Biometrics offers a great key to safekeeping. Conventional biometrics system for person authentication is based on two mechanisms such as verification and identification. Verification deals with one-to-one matching whereas identification ensures one-to-many matching.

1.1 Introduction to Biometrics

Ross et al. (2003), described biometrics as "Any automatically measurable, robust and distinctive physical characteristic or personal trait that can be used to identify an individual or verify the claimed identity of an individual". Jain et al. (2004) defined biometrics as the system used for human recognition consisting of *identification* and *verification* along with their advantages, disadvantages, and some challenges.

1.2 Need for Biometrics

Generally, people used passwords, keys, or PINs (personal identification numbers) for person verification or identification but it has many drawbacks such as; the password may be forgotten or hacked; PINs may be stolen, or cards may be lost or stolen.

Biometrics offers the solution to these problems, now person identification and verification by biometrics are so easy and highly secure.

Biometric technologies are developed based on recognizing the characteristics of a person. Biometrics is a very useful technique used in numerous applications. Examples of biometrics include the face, Ear, Palm recognition, fingerprint matching, DNA matching, iris recognition, speech recognition, gait recognition, etc.

1.3 Challenges in Biometrics

Some of the challenges commonly encountered in the implementation of biometric systems are given as:

- **Intra-class variations**: These variations are typically caused by a user incorrectly interacting with the sensor, such as an incorrect facial pose, or when the characteristics of a sensor are altered during authentication.
- **Noise:** A biometric data set captured by an image acquisition system or sensor may be influenced by noise signals introduced by the sensor itself. This could be due to poor acquisition conditions. Subtle variations in the biometric itself, such as a fingerprint image with a scar or a voice sample altered by cold, could also contribute to noise. Noisy data can also be caused by faulty or improperly maintained sensors, such as dirt accumulation on a fingerprint sensor, or by unfavorable ambient conditions, such as poor lighting.
- **Spoof attacks**: When behavioral traits such as signature or voice are used, this type of attack is relevant. Physical characteristics, such as fingerprints, are, however, vulnerable to spoofing attacks.

- **Non-universality**: A subset of users may be unable to provide meaningful biometric data to the biometric system. Due to the poor quality of the ridges, a fingerprint biometric system may extract incorrect niceties features from certain individuals' fingerprints.

CHAPTER 2

BIOMETRIC MODALITIES

Biometrics or biometric security technology uses some characteristics known as biometric modalities; which can be classified as physiological and behavioral modalities. The biometric modalities are also referred to as biometric traits. Jain et al. (2006) opined that all biometric verifiers may be considered combinations of physiological and behavioral characteristics due to the interaction between the user and the system. Some of the modalities are related to the physical structure or properties of the human body, and some other traits are associated with human behavior. A few examples of physiological and behavioral traits are:

2.1 Physiological Traits: Physical characteristics of human beings such as the face, hand, hand geometry, fingerprints, ear shapes, iris or retina characteristics, etc. are called physiological traits. A few of the traits of the same person are shown in Figure 2.1.

2.1.1 Face biometrics: Face recognition technology is a method of identifying a person based on features extracted from the person's face. This is a computer application that uses a digital image or a video frame captured to identify an individual or verify a person. This is the most commonly used type of biometric system. There are several types of face recognition methods that use facial metrics and Eigen's faces. The facial metric method is based on specific facial features such as the positioning of the eyes, nose, and mouth, as well as the distance between these features.

(a) Face

2.1.2 Ear biometrics: The ear is used as a modality in-ear biometrics, where features or character traits of the ear are used as the basis of similarity. This is a consistent biometric system that does not change with age. The human ear is another visible part of the body that can be used for a noninvasive biometric technique. From infancy to adulthood, the ears undergo very minor changes. The ears, like the face, do not change appearance as a result of hair growth.

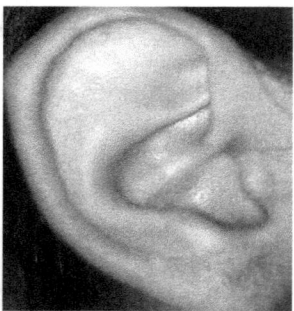

(b)Ear

2.1.3 Fingerprint biometrics: A fingerprint is a pattern formed by the ridges and valleys of finger and thumb images. A friction ridge is a raised portion of the palmer (palm), digits (fingers and toes), or plantar (sole) skin that is composed of one or more connected ridge units of friction ridge skin. The traditional method involves the use of ink to transfer the fingerprint to a piece of paper. In the modern approach, fingerprint readers or scanners based on optical, thermal, silicon, or ultrasonic concepts are used. The most common type of fingerprint reader is an optical fingerprint reader, which is based on changes in reflection at the points where finger lines touch the surface.

(c) Finger

2.1.4 Footprint biometrics: Footprint identification is the process of measuring footprint features in order to identify a person. The footprint is universal, simple to capture, and does not change significantly over time. A fingerprint biometric system does not necessitate the use of specialized acquisition devices. For each person, a footprint image of a left/right leg is captured from various angles. This setup makes no use of any special lighting.

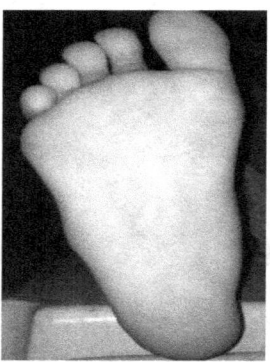

(d)Foot

2.1.5 Hand Geometry biometrics: This is based on characteristics of the hand geometry of persons. Every person's hand is shaped differently and a person's hand does not change after a certain age. The methods include the estimation of length, width, thickness, and surface area of the hand. Various methods are used to measure the hand geometry using mechanical or optical principles.

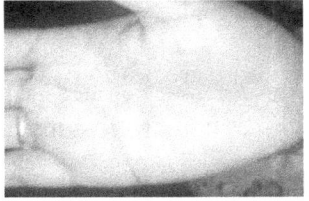

(f) Plam print

2.1.6 Iris biometrics: The iris of the eye, which is a colored area that isometrically surrounds the pupil, is used for iris recognition. Iris patterns are one-of-a-kind and can only be obtained using a suitable image acquisition system. Each iris structure has a unique pattern. Corona, crypts, filaments, freckles, pits, furrows, striations, and rings are examples of specific characteristics. Despite the fact that biometrics is not very user-friendly, it provides optimal performance.

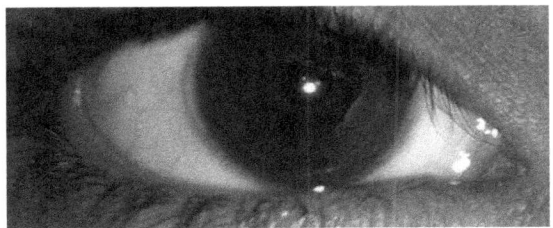

(e) Eye highlighting iris of a person

Fig.2.1 Physiological traits of a person

2.2 Behavioral Traits: The characteristics associated with the behavior of persons are known as behavioral traits such as signature, voice, keystroke, gait pattern, etc. shown in figure2.2.

2.2.1 Voice biometrics: Every person's voice has a different pitch, and this is regarded as a behavioral trait. Voice recognition is primarily based on the analysis of how people speak. Voice recognition, also known as speaker recognition, is a type of speech recognition that focuses on the vocal characteristics that produce speech rather than the sound or pronunciation of the speech itself. The dimensions of the vocal tract, mouth, nasal cavities, and other speech processing mechanisms in the human body influence vocal characteristics. These biometrics do not necessitate any specialized or expensive hardware.

(a) Speech recognization

2.2.2 Signature biometrics: Signature recognition is based on the dynamics of signing. The dynamics of signature are measured using pressure, direction, acceleration, stroke length, dynamic number of strokes, and duration. The most obvious and significant advantage of this is that a fraudster cannot learn how to write a signature by simply looking at one that has already been written. To capture the signature dynamics, various devices are used. These are either standard tablets or specialized devices.

(b) Signature

2.2.3 Keystroke biometrics: Keystroke is a method of verifying an individual's identity based on the personality types and uses keystrokes on the keyboard. The typing rhythm, which can accommodate both trained and amateur two-finger typists, is critical in this type of biometrics.

(c) Keystroke

Fig.2.2 Behavioral traits of a person

CHAPTER 3

BIOMETRIC AUTHENTICATION SYSTEM

A biometric-based authentication system operates in two modes identification and verification.

Identification deals with one-to-many matching; whereas verification is one-to-one, which means that verification can result in who the person is among the persons present in the database. Identification authenticates a person and ensures the presence or absence of a person but it does not report the exact identity of the person.

3.1 Enrolment Process

Enrolment is a very important process involved in biometrics. This is illustrated in figure 3.1 The steps of biometric trait enrolment are:

- A suitable acquisition system or sensor is used to capture the biometric data or input.
- The modality is kept in the biometric database.

- Features are extracted from traits and converted into appropriate transformations known as biometric templates.

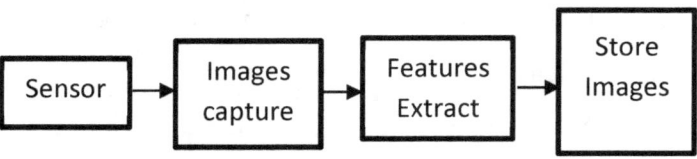

Fig.3.1 Enrollment process

3.2 Training involved in Biometric System

A biometric system is divided into two major processes namely training and testing. During the training process, biometric modality is captured and converted into a suitable template. This process is performed as:
- The image or signal input is captured or acquired.
- The signal is pre-processed to remove noise or other similar signals, or image resizing and reformatting occur.
- Feature extraction is carried out.

- Features are transformed into appropriate templates, which are then saved in the template database.

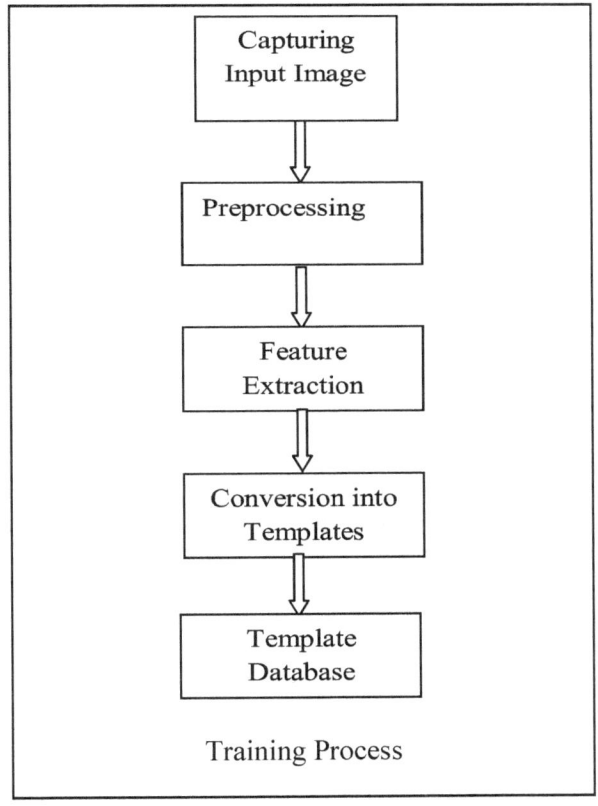

Fig. 3.2 Training process involved in biometrics

3.3 Testing involved in Biometric System

The testing process is performed at the time of matching, which is similar to the training method.

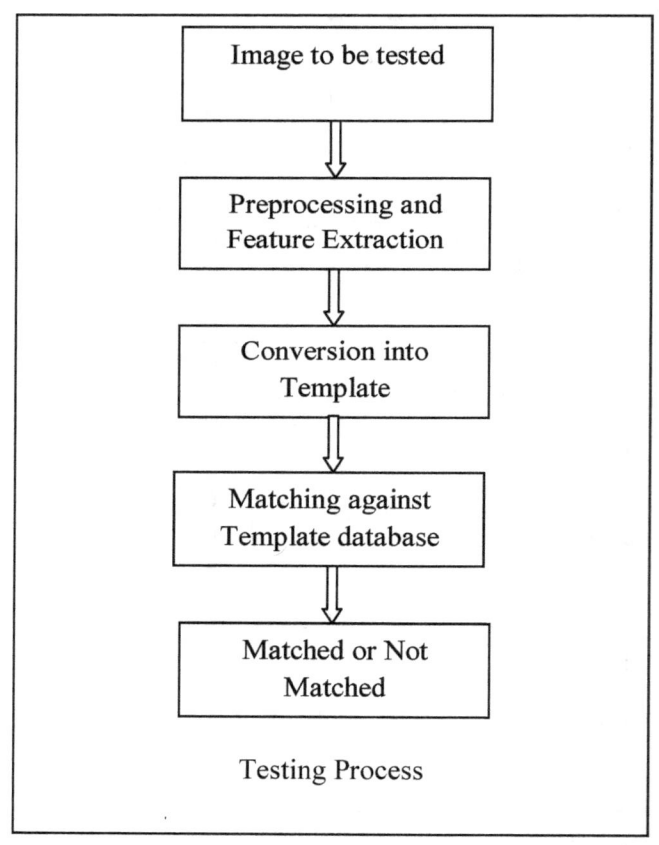

Fig. 3.3 Testing process involved in biometrics

The template is compared to the templates already in the template databases. If there is a match, it
The input is recorded and subjected to the following procedures:
- Pre-processing.
- Extraction of features.
- Conversion of a template

The output matches the input. Figures 3.2 and 3.3 depict the training and testing processes, respectively.

CHAPTER 4

MULTIMODAL BIOMETRICS SYSTEM

4.1 Multimodal Biometrics

According to Jain et al. (2004), the term "multimodal" refers to combining two or more different biometric sources of a person, such as a person's face, ear, iris, and foot sensed by different sensors. Multiple sources of biometric information are combined to overcome some of the limitations mentioned in Ross et al. unimodal's biometric system (2007). According to Jing et al. (2007), most biometric systems used in real-world applications are unimodal and rely on evidence from a single source of information for authentication, such as a fingerprint, face, voice, and so on. These systems are vulnerable to a wide range of issues, including noisy data, intra-class variations, inter-class similarities, non-universality, and spoofing. Figure 4.1 depicts a typical example of multimodal biometrics.

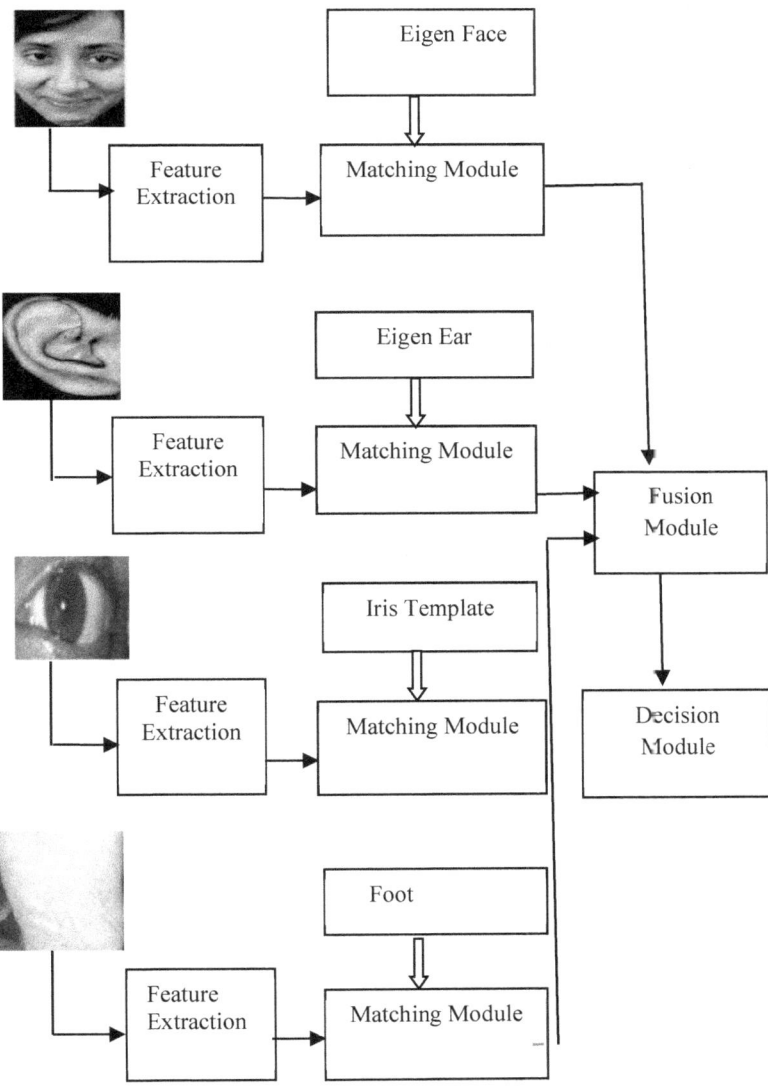

Fig. 4.1 Multimodal Biometric system

These modalities could be combined at various levels as shown in the figure. The fusion can be applied at matching score level, feature level, or decision level; as discussed in the next section briefly.

4.2 Architecture of Unimodal Biometrics System

If one modality is involved then it becomes a Unimodal biometrics system.

Uni-modal Biometric System

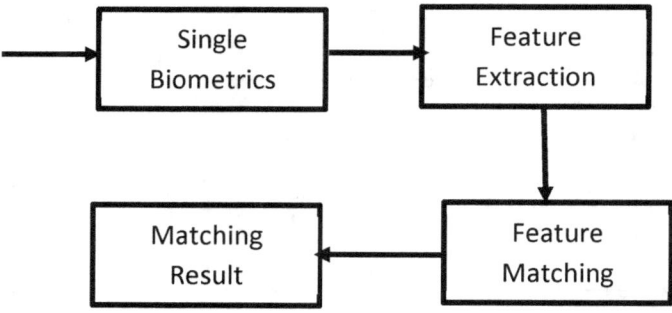

Fig.4.2 Architecture of Unimodal Biometrics System

figure 4.2 depicts a process of unimodal biometrics, with the example of face recognition highlighted. The image of the face is enrolled, pre-processed, and features extracted and saved in the template database. The test facial image is now compared to the one in the database. If there is a template available in the database, matching occurs.

4.3 Architecture of Multimodal Biometrics System

If more than one modality is involved then it becomes a multimodal biometrics system.

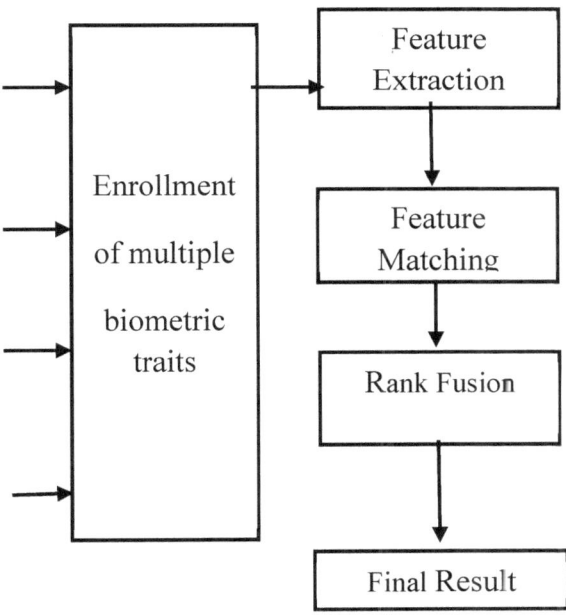

Fig.4.3 Architecture of Multimodal Biometrics System

Figure 4.3 depicts an example of multimodal biometrics. One of the main tasks for a multimodal biometric system is the selection of appropriate biometric traits, which is dependent on several factors such as the type of biometric operation, namely identification or verification, perceived risks, user type, and need for security. The primary goal is to assess the performance of the multimodal biometric system based on various levels of fusion using various classifier approaches and techniques.

4.4 Drawbacks of Unimodal biometric System

Biometrics based on a single trait or characteristic are very simple and easy to apply. These biometric systems, however, have the following major drawbacks:

- Some characteristics do not have universal applicability.
- Noisy signals captured by sensors as a result of incorrect usage and environmental conditions such as humidity, dirt, dust, and so on.
- The discrimination of biometric systems as a result of high in-class variability and low inter-class variability.

- The performance of unimodal systems in recognition is limited to a certain level.
- Error rates are occasionally unacceptable.
- The biometric characteristics' lack of permanence and variability.
- The possibility of fraud through cloning, either voluntarily or involuntarily.
- If there are issues with the trait being used, there are no alternatives that could save the biometric system.

CHAPTER 5

FUSION LEVELS AND TECHNIQUES

5.1 Introduction to Fusion levels

A multimodal biometric system can be designed by integrating several modalities using different fusion schemes. The main goal of fusion is to determine the best set of expert values that can optimally combine the decisions rendered by the individual experts. There are several types of fusion schemes in literature used in multimodal biometrics. A brief description of the fusion methods is presented here.

Multimodal biometrics system involves various levels of fusion. The main aim of using fusion is to determine the best set of experts in a problem domain and devise an appropriate function that could combine the decisions of individual experts at an optimum level. These are categorized as:

- Before matching
- After matching

5.1.1 Fusion Level Before matching

Fusion schemes before matching are used to integrate the evidence before matching. Sensor level and feature level fusion are important fusion schemes under this category.

- **Sensor level:** The raw data acquired from multiple sensors can be processed and combined to generate new data from which features can be extracted. The raw data obtained as different modalities from sensors are fused. Ross et al. (2006) suggested that the sensor level fusion can be performed if the data or modalities are obtained from multiple compatible sensors or multiple instances of the same biometric trait obtain using a single sensor. Since sensor level fusion combines the information from a different sensor, it requires some pre-processing such as sensor calibration and data registration before performing the fusion.

- **Feature level:** The feature sets extracted from multiple data sources can be combined to create a new feature set to represent the individual. The geometric features of the hand may be augmented with the Eigen coefficients of the face to construct a new high-dimensional feature vector. Feature level fusion consolidates the features obtained from different modalities using suitable methods of feature extraction. Ross et al. (2006) stated that if the features are structurally compatible then the features can be combined and this is done by using the features obtained from different sources. This approach also introduces a curse of dimensionality and hence either feature transformation or feature selection can be applied to reduce the dimensionality of the fused feature set.

5.1.2 Fusion Level After Matching

Fusion schemes after matching are used to combine pieces of evidence after matching. This type of fusion includes the following:

- **Match Score level:** Multiple classifier's result scores are combined to generate a single scalar score. The match scores generated by the face and hand modalities of a user may be combined using a simple sum rule to obtain a new match score which is then used to make the final decision. Match score is a measure of the similarity between the input and template biometric feature vector. Ross et al. (2006) described in match score level fusion, the match score obtained from different matches are combined. Since scores obtained from different matches are not homogeneous, the score normalization technique maps the scores obtained from different matcher onto the same range.
- **Decision level:** When the fusion is at the decision level then each matcher output is combined to accept or reject in a verification system. Decision level fusion involves the fusion of decisions obtained using different modalities. Since decision level fusion holds the binary value it is also called abstract level fusion. The strategy adopted for the

concatenation of biometric modalities depends on the level at which fusion is performed. Fusion at the feature level can be accomplished by concatenating two compatible feature sets. Feature selection/reduction techniques may be employed to handle the curse-of-dimensionality problem.

- **Rank level:** This type of fusion is relevant in identification systems where each classifier associates a rank with every enrolled identity.

Duin et al. (2000) studied the fusion at the match score level. Verlinde et al. (1999) stated in the context of verification that two distinct strategies exist for fusion at this level. In the first approach, the fusion is viewed as a classification problem where a feature vector is constructed using the matching scores output by the individual matches. Then this feature vector is classified into one of two classes: Accept (genuine user) or Reject (impostor). Dieckmann et al. (1997) described the second approach the fusion is viewed as a combination problem where the individual matching scores are combined to generate a single scalar score which is then used to make the final decision.

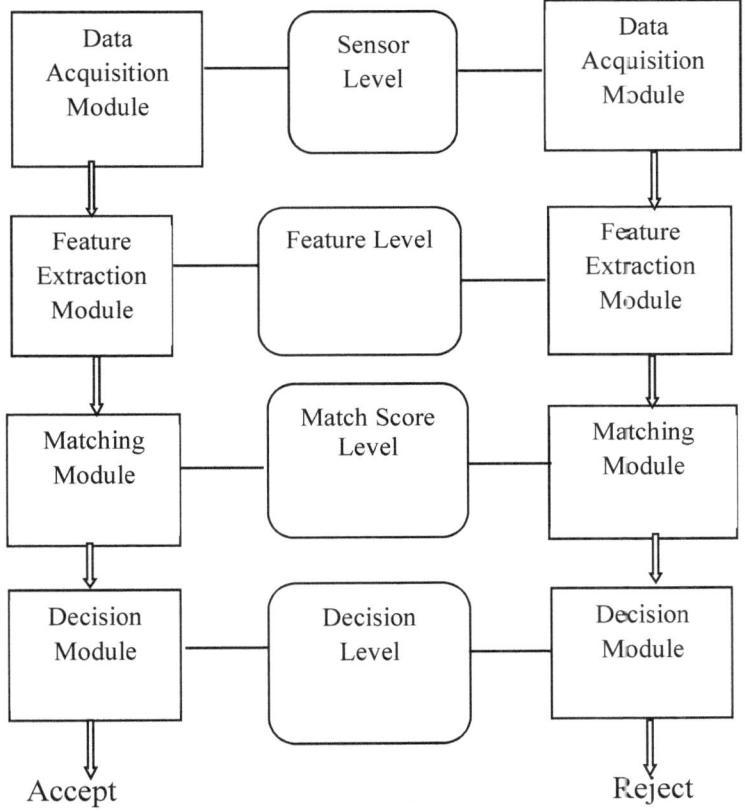

Fig. 5.1 Different Fusion Schemes

Ross et al. (2003) demonstrated that the simple sum rule is sufficient to significantly improve the matching performance of a multimodal biometric system.

There are difficulties with sensor level and feature level fusion because these schemes require the data acquired by different sensors as compatible and feature set obtained by different traits may either be inaccessible or incompatible. Fusion at the matching score level is the most preferred because it has sufficient information and can be easily combined and accessible.

5.2 The Fusion Technique

A decision made by a biometric system is either "genuine" or "impostor." For each type of decision, there are two possible outcomes: true or false. As a result, there are four possible outcomes: a genuine individual is accepted or a genuine match occurred, a genuine individual is rejected or a false rejection occurred, an impostor is rejected or a genuine rejection occurred, and an impostor is accepted or a false match occurred. All biometric traits (face, ear, Iris, and foot) were acquired and subjected to biometrics. The genuine score, impostor score, False Accept Rate (FAR), and False Reject Rate (FRR) were calculated. The ERR/ROC (error/region of convergence) curve was plotted against FAR at various points. At a matching score level, the matching module compares extracted features against the stored templates to generate a match score in verification mode. In verification mode, the system validates a person's identity by comparing the captured biometric data with his biometric template stored in the system database. We have prepared the database for all biometric traits like face, ear, iris, and foot. A few major score values are given below.

- **Genuine score:** A match score is considered genuine if it is the result of matching two samples of biometric traits from the same user. A genuine score is one that falls below a predefined threshold.
- **Imposter score:** If a score is an imposter score, it is the result of matching two samples of a biometric trait from different users. An imposter

score is defined as one that exceeds the predefined threshold.

FAR, FRR, and other important parameters are used in performance evaluation.

- **False accept rate (FAR):** The probability of an impostor being accepted as a genuine individual is defined as the false accept rate. The FAR is calculated by assuming that the rate of several people is incorrectly accepted in relation to the total number of enrolled people.

- **False reject rate (FRR):** The probability of an impostor being accepted as a genuine individual is defined as the false accept rate. The FAR is calculated by assuming that the rate of several people is incorrectly accepted in relation to the total number of enrolled people.

- **Relative Operating Characteristic (ROC):** By adjusting some parameters, the values of FAR and FRR can be traded off against each other. The ROC plotted as a graph against the values of FAR and FRR, with the variables changed implicitly.

- **Equal Error Rate (EER):** EER is the rate at which both accept and reject errors are equal. The ERR is commonly used when a quick comparison of two systems is required. This is obtained from the ROC at the point where FAR and FRR are equal. The system's accuracy improves as the EER decreases.
- **Weight of biometric traits:** The experiment's fusion technique is based on the different weights assigned to each biometric trait. Wti, the weight for the ith trait, is calcul:

$$Wt_i = \frac{1}{EER_i}$$

- **Normalized score:** Individual trait match scores may not be homogeneous, and match scores at the output of different traits may follow different statistical distributions. As a result, the Min-Max normalisation technique is used to compute each trait's normalised score. A normalised score is used to calculate the weight of a specific trait among all biometric traits:

$$Wt_i = \frac{\frac{1}{EER_i}}{\sum_{j=1}^{n} \frac{1}{EER_j}}$$

where EER_j is the equal error rate for the jth trait and 'n' is the number of traits.

- **Score after fusion:** The sum rule-based fusion is used in the work. The score after fusion is calculated as:

$$S = \sum_{j=1}^{n}(W_j S_j)$$

where S_j is match score and W_j is the weight of jth trait respectively.

5.3 Normalization Technique

Normalization is required in combining the scores of different traits into a single score because the match scores at the output of the individual trait may not be homogeneous. If the scores are not similar then it becomes very difficult to combine various scores. The range of score values may also not be the same for all the modalities. To address these disparities, normalization techniques are used. Normalization of the score is necessary to transform the scores of each trait into a common score value. Min-Max normalization technique has been used in the work where the minimum and maximum bounds of the scores produced by a particular trait to 0 and 1 are shifted. If the matching score of a particular trait is not bounded then minimum and maximum values are found from the training set of match scores of that particular trait. Let' and 'y' be the matching score before and after normalization, respectively. The Min-Max technique computes the value of 'y' as:

$$y = \frac{x - \min(S_x)}{\max(S_x) - \min(S_x)}$$

where S_x is the set of all possible matching scores generated by a particular modality.

Min-Max normalization retains the original distribution of scores and transforms all the scores into a common range [0, 1].

CHAPTER 6

FACE RECOGNITION

6.1 Face Recognition

The multimodal biometrics employs recognisable facial characteristics of faces and important features as templates. The templates are feature transformations that are equivalent. The templates are compared to a previously known training set of face images. Faces are fed into the system, and using Principal Component Analysis (PCA), features are extracted and saved in the template database.

The result is a reconstructed image based on face matching using the minimum Euclidian distance. A face recognition process is depicted in Figure 6.1. Faces are recognised using features extracted from the faces in order to represent the faces. Feature vectors are used to store features. There have been numerous research contributions to the extraction of facial image features. Belhumeur et al. (1997) proposed a few successful appearance-based approaches. and processing the images as two-dimensional (2-D) patterns.

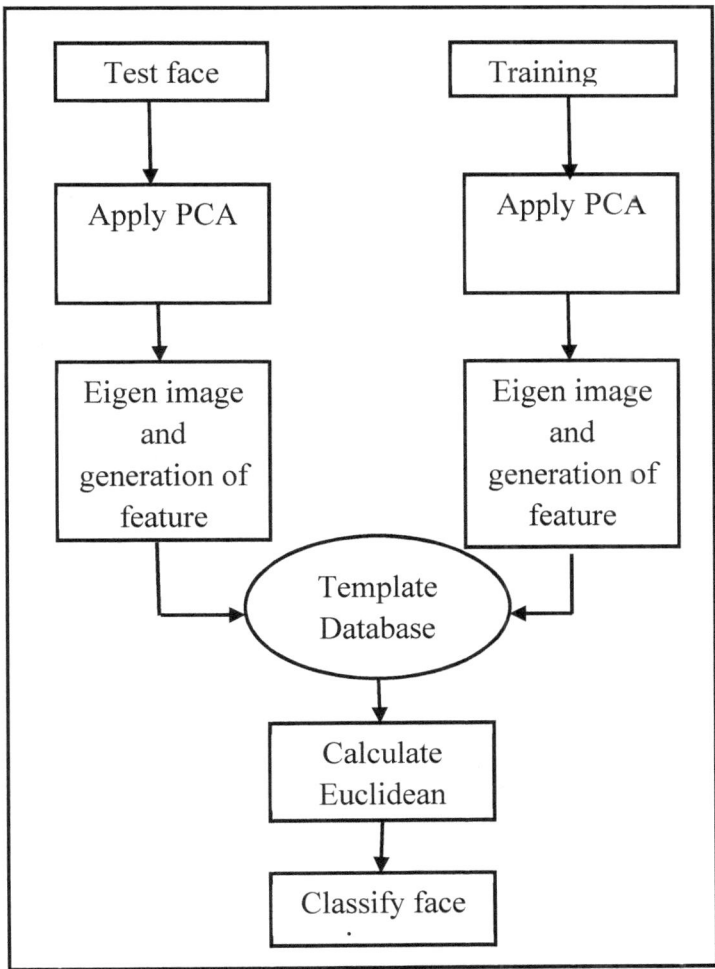

Fig. 6.1 Face recognition process

6.2 Principal Component Analysis

Principal Component Analysis is the most widely used algorithm in face recognition methods (PCA). The algorithm's main concept is to de-correlate data to obtain differences and similarities by locating the principal directions, which are Eigenvectors of the covariance matrix of multidimensional data. To begin, the system is loaded with a training set of face image vectors containing images of each subject. The biometric system is tested using face images from the training set of face images. The images are then trained to generate Eigenvectors using PCA and a training set of images. The mean image is calculated as follows:

$$\psi_{Train} = \frac{1}{M}\sum_{n-1}^{M}\Gamma_n \qquad (1)$$

where ψ_i is the mean subtracted image.

The image ψ_i can be obtained by:

$$\psi_i = \Gamma_i - \psi_{Train} \quad i = 1,2,\ldots..M \qquad (2)$$

It is a large vector set subjected to PCA to get a set of M orthonormal vectors, Un. The kth vector, U_k, is selected as:

$$\lambda_K = \frac{1}{M} \sum_{n-1}^{M}(U_k^T \Phi_n)^2 \qquad (3)$$

where vectors U_k and scalars λ_k are the Eigenvectors and Eigenvalues respectively.

The covariance matrix (CM) is given as:

$$CM = \frac{1}{M}\sum_{n-1}^{M}(\Phi_n\Phi_n^T) = AA^T \qquad (4)$$

The mean image Ψ is computed and projected onto the "face space" by the M Eigen vectors, resulting in:

$$\omega_K = U_K^T \Phi_i \quad K = 1 \ldots M \qquad (5)$$

The distance between the projections is calculated by the Euclidean distance between the training and test classification space projections as:

$$D_K = \parallel \Omega - \Omega_k \parallel \qquad (6)$$

where k^{th} face class is described by DK vector.

Each image in the training set is transformed into image space and its constituents are saved in memory. The system processes an input face and projects it onto the face space. The Euclidian distance is then calculated. It is necessary to determine whether the image presented to the system is facing or not. to be checked. Figure 6.2 shows a training set of faces images and Figure 6.3 shows equivalent Eigenfaces.

Fig. 6.2 Training set of faces

Fig. 6.3 Eigenfaces of facial images of the image database

CHAPTER 7

EAR RECOGNITION

7.1 Ear Recognition

The human ear is a relatively new class of biometrics, similar to how the face is a visible part of the human body that can be used for a non-invasive biometric technique. The ear is a good example of a stable biometric that does not change with age. As illustrated in Figure 7.1, the ear does not have a completely random structure.

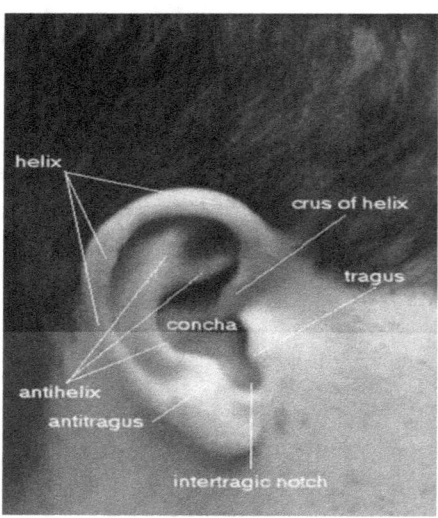

Fig. 7.1 Anatomy of the ear

Several methods are described in the existing biometric system literature. Ear databases of various people were created for the proposed multimodal system. The database contains images of ears with varying lighting and orientation. The Eigen image algorithm has been released for ear recognition. The steps for creating Eigen's ears are similar to those for creating Eigen's faces. Chang et al. (2003) used a standard PCA algorithm for ear recognition and concluded that there isn't much of a difference in recognition rate between the ear and the face. The ear recognition system is depicted in Figure 7.2.

7.2 Eigen Image

Darwish et al. (2009) identified the Eigen image method as the most effective method for face recognition systems, and it could also be used in ear biometrics. The ear recognition process is started by using the training set of ear images. The images of the side faces were also captured with the high-quality camera in the same lighting conditions. Using a pre-processing operation, the rear portion is cropped from the side face image. The colour images are converted to grayscale images before being subjected to subsequent biometric stages.

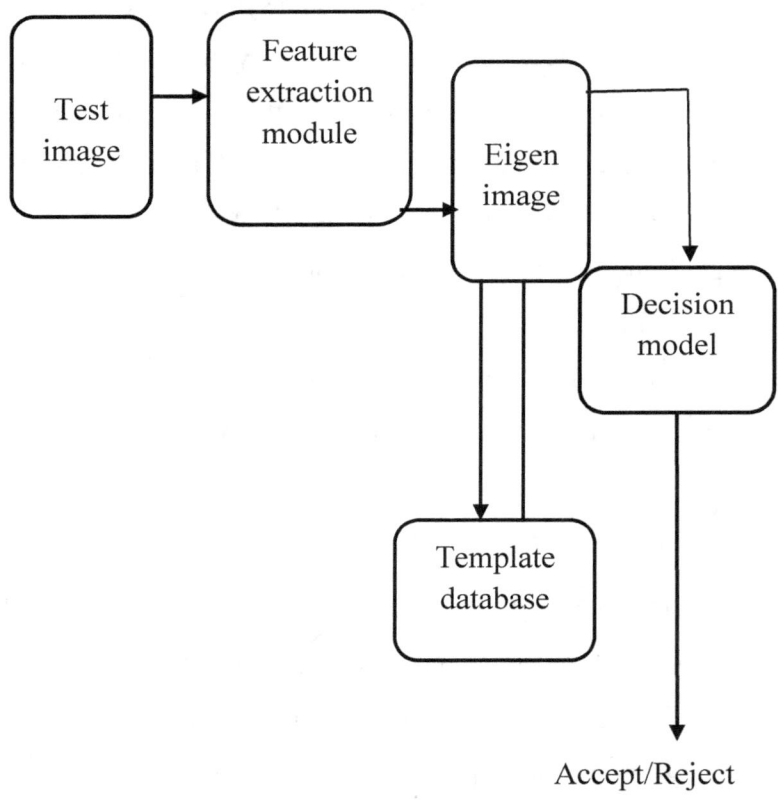

Fig. 7.2 Ear recognition system

Figure 7.3 depicts a dataset of grayscale images obtained by cropping the image's ear portion. Each image set contains images from both the training and test sets. An ear image can be thought of as a vector in a massive dimensional space with concatenating columns. The proposed method is based on pre-processed normalized ear images. The images' covariance matrix is then used to compute Eigenvectors and Eigenvalues.

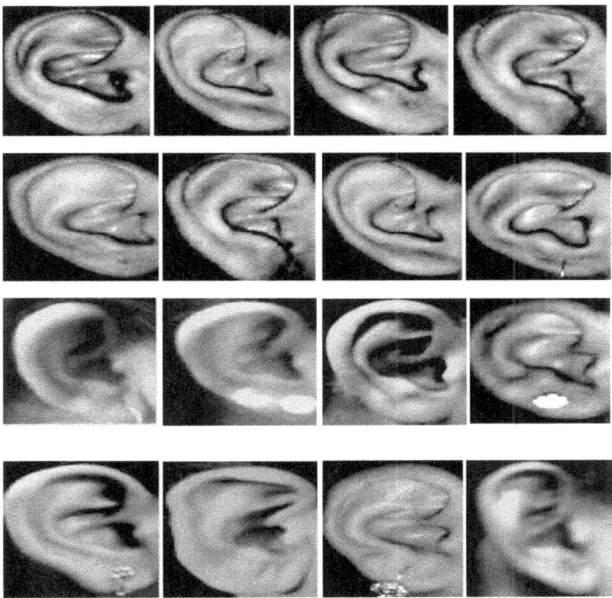

Fig. 7.3 Grayscale images of ears

The weights of the ear images are stored and projected onto the image space. The test image is projected into the Eigenspace once the Eigenspace has been defined. Images that have a low correlation can be rejected. A threshold is used to determine acceptance or rejection; the distance below the threshold is a match. Figure 7.4 depicts the ear image results as Eigen images.

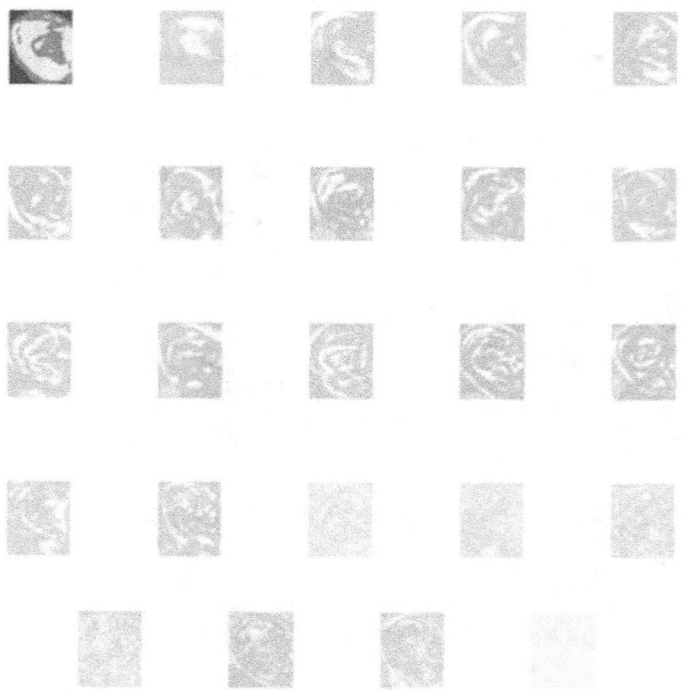

Fig. 7.4 Eigen images of ears

CHAPTER 8

IRIS RECOGNITION

8.1 Iris Recognition

The iris of an eye is a visible ring structure that surrounds the pupil of the eyes. It is a muscular structure that controls the amount of light entering an eye. Iris recognition system is supposed to be the most accurate biometrics that utilizes the measurable features of the iris. Figure 8.1 shows an eye highlighting the iris and other parts.

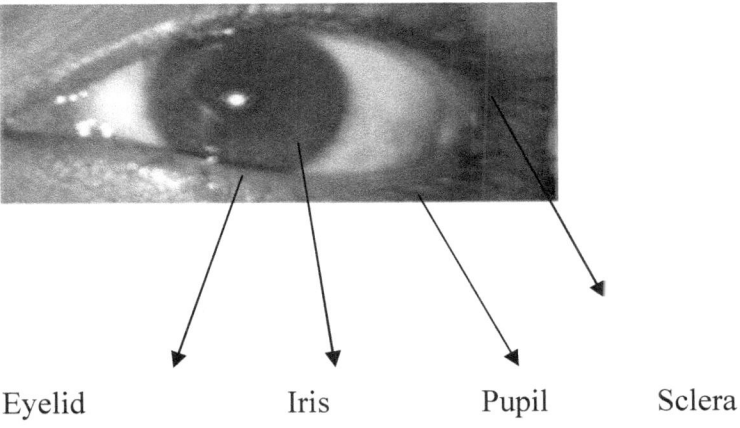

Fig. 8.1 Human eye highlighting iris and other parts

Hamming distance method was introduced by Hamming et al. (1950); which has been used in iris recognition in the proposed work. The iris images are cropped from the eyes and then applied to pre-processing and encoding with Hough transform, as defined by Hough et al. (1962). The iris parts are localized of the eye image and outside the pupil using an automatic segmentation algorithm based on the Hough transform. The Hough transform method is a general-purpose method for identifying the locations and orientations of features in a digital image. The method is simple, easy to implement, handles missing and occluded data, and can be adapted to many types of forms, not just lines. As the iris has edges with a known shape as a circle, using the Hough transform is feasible for detecting and linking edges to form closed iris areas.

8.2 Segmentation

The Iris region is segmented from the eye image and it is approximated by two circles, indicating the iris boundary and pupil boundary respectively. The eyelids and eyelashes are the upper and lower parts of the iris region. Kong et al. (2001) presented a method for eyelash detection, where eyelashes are treated as separable eyelashes, which are isolated in the image, and multiple eyelashes, which are bunched together and overlap in the eye image. Separable eyelashes are detected using 1D Gabor filters since the convolution of a separable eyelash with the secular reflections along the eye image are detected using a threshold. The intensity values at these regions will be higher than at any other regions in the image. The most popular computer vision algorithm is Hough transform which is used for geometric shapes like lines and circles in an object. The circular Hough transform can be used to detect iris regions' radius and center coordinates. Wildes et al. (1994) developed an automated iris recognition system. Kong et al. (2001) suggested an accurate iris segmentation method based on a novel reflection and eyelash detection model. An individual is identified using human iris recognition. The parameters used are the center coordinates x_c and y_c, and the radius r. A maximum point in the Hough space will correspond to the radius and center coordinates of the circle best defined by the edge points. The eyelid is detected by the horizontal direction and the outer circular boundary of the iris is detected by vertical direction derivatives. A rubber sheet model is used as shown in Figure 6.7 to remap each point within the iris region to a pair of polar coordinates ((r, θ), where r lies in the interval [0,1] and θ is the angular variable, cyclic over [0,2π]. This remapping of the iris region can be modeled as,

$$I(x(r,\theta), y(r,\theta)) \rightarrow I(r,\theta) \qquad (1)$$

where $x(r,\theta) = (1-r)\, x_p(\theta) + r x_i(\theta)$; $y(r,\theta) = (1-r) y_p(\theta) + r y_i(\theta)$.; *I(x, y)* is the iris region image; *(x, y)* is the original Cartesian coordinates; *(r, θ)* are the corresponding normalized polar coordinates; and *(x$_p$, y$_p$)* and *(x$_i$, y$_i$)* are the coordinates of the pupil and iris boundaries along the *θ* direction respectively. The transformed pattern produces a 2D array with horizontal dimensions of angular resolution and vertical dimensions of radial resolution.

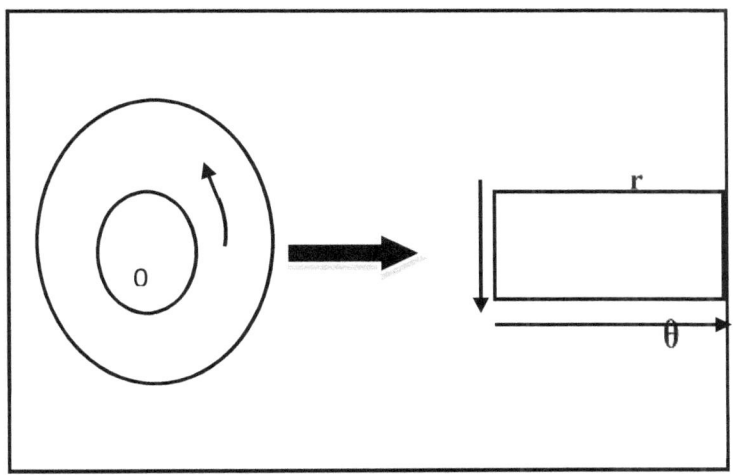

Fig. 8.2 The rubber sheet model

8.3 Normalization and Encoding

After successful iris region segmentation, the segmented region is transformed to convert into dimensions. The dimensional inconsistencies between eye images are mainly due to the stretching of the iris caused by pupil dilation from varying levels of illumination. The normalization process will producan e iris region having same constant dimensions. The homogenous rubber sheet model suggested by Daugman et al. (1988) remaps each point within the iris region to a pair of polar coordinates (r,θ) where r is on the interval [0, 1] and θ is angle [0,2π]. In this system, rotation is accounted for during matching by shifting the iris templates in the direction until two iris templates are aligned. Figure 8.3 shows a grayscale cropped iris image and the iris after segmentation is shown in Figure 8.4.

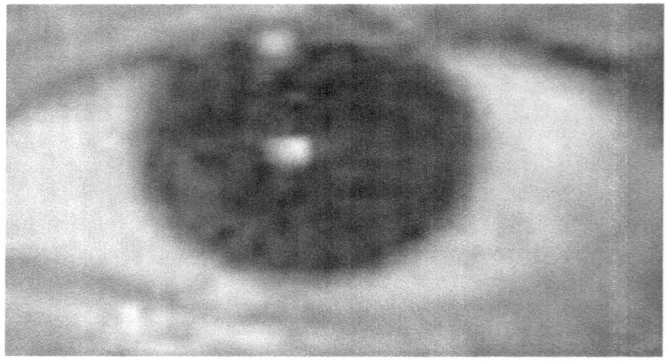

Fig. 8.3 Cropped and grayscale image of the eye

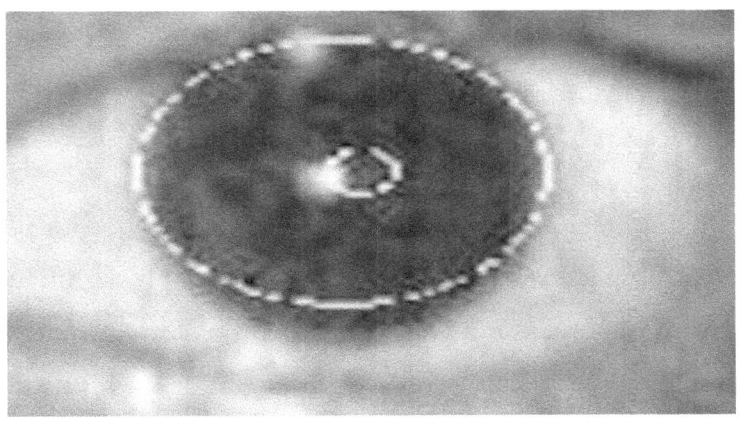

Fig. 8.4 Segmented iris region

Encoding of features extracted from the iris region is achieved by convolving the normalized iris pattern with 1D Log-Gabor wavelets. The 2D normalized pattern is broken up into numbers of 1D signals. These 1D signals are convolved with 1D Gabor wavelets. The rows of the 2D normalized pattern are taken as the 1D signal; each row corresponds to a circular ring on the iris region. The intensity values at known noise areas in the normalized pattern are set to the average intensity of surrounding pixels to prevent the influence of noise in the output of the filtering. The output of filtering is phase quantized to four levels with each filter producing two bits of data for each phase.

8.4 Iris Matching

Hamming distance is chosen as a metric for recognition as a distance measure. The Hamming distance s calculated best templates by using only important bits. These bits in the iris pattern that corresponds to '0' bits in noise masks of both iris patterns will be used in the calculation. Thee considers only the bits generated from the accurate iris region, and this is modified by each template. The Hamming distance (HD) between two Boolean iris vectors is defined as:

$$HD = \frac{||C_A \otimes C_B \cap M_A \cap M_B||}{||M_A \cap M_B||} \qquad (2)$$

where, C_A and C_B are the coefficients of two iris images respectively; and M_A and M_B are the mask image of two iris images respectively. The $\otimes$ is the XOR operator which shows difference between a corresponding pair of bits, and $\cap$ is the AND operator which shows the compared bits. The denominator of the above equation is used to reduce the effect of the unwanted portion of the iris due to eyelashes or eyelids. Ideally, the Hamming distance of two irises should be 0.

CHAPTER 9

FOOT RECOGNITION

9.1 Foot Recognition

Footprint identification deals with the measurement of footprint features for the recognition of the identity of a person. The footprint is universal, easy to capture, and does not change much across time. Footprint biometric system does not require specialized acquisition devices. A footprint image of a left/right leg is captured of people in different angles. No special lighting is used in this setup. Footprint texture features are usually extracted using transform-based method such as Fourier Transform (Wenxin et al. (2002)) and Discrete Cosine Transform (Jing, et al. (2004)). Wavelet Transform was also introduced by Qian et al. (2002) which is also used to extract the texture features of the footprint. Figure 9.1 shows the footprint recognition process.

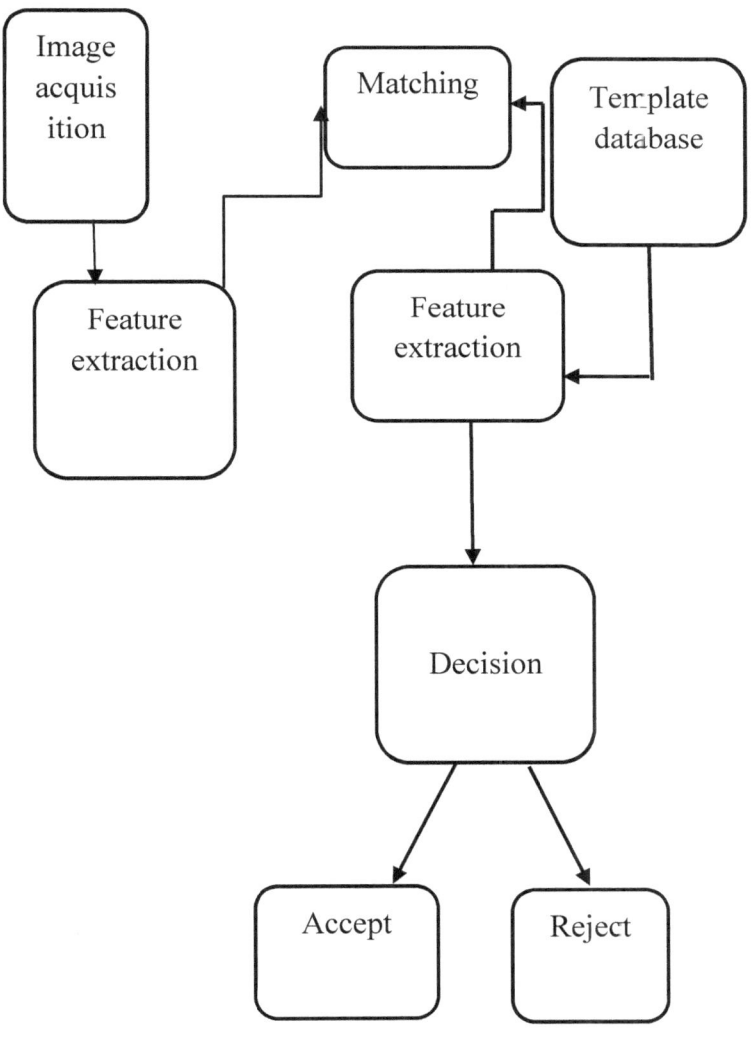

Fig. 9.1 Footprint biometric system

A footprint-based personal recognition method is used where the foot image is positioned and cropped according to the key points. Then, a sequential modified Haar Wavelet is proposed to find the modified Haar Energy (MHE) feature. Figure 9.2 shows the proposed footprint identification using sequential modified Haar Transform.

9.2 Sequential Modified Haar Wavelet Transform Method

Foot image features are extracted by transform-based method like Discrete Cosine Transform and Fourier transform. Wenxin et al. (2002) suggested that Fourier transform has floating-valued signals that involve into integer-valued signals giving less accuracy, and Jing et al. (2004) observed in Discrete Cosine Transform that some points are missed leading to incorrect inference. Qian et al. (2002) introduced another transform method wavelet transform which is used to take out the features of the foot image.

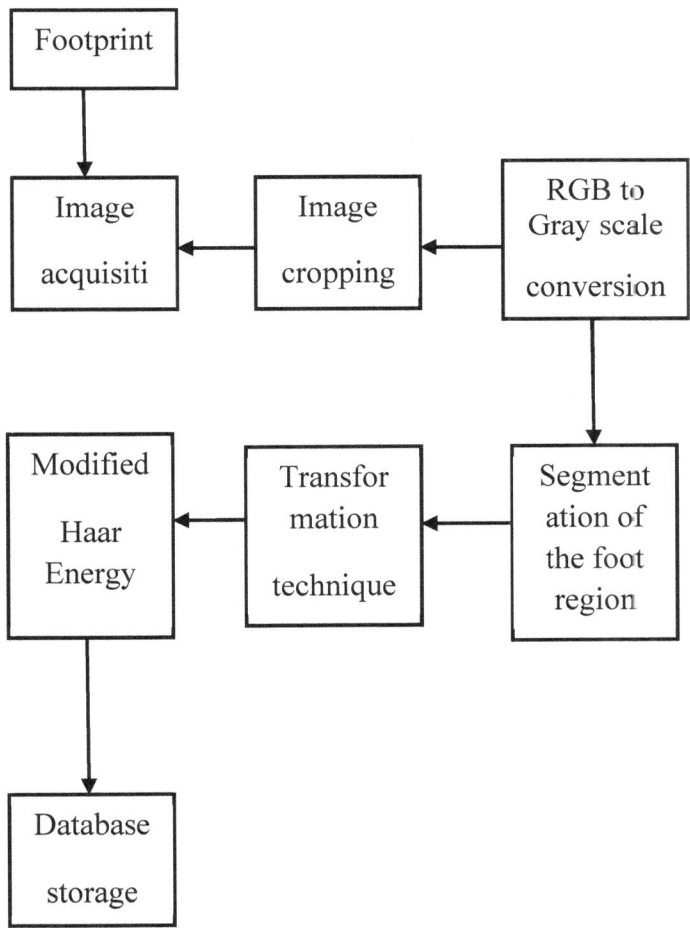

Fig. 9.2 Footprint identification system

modified Haar transform is applied to the resize footprint image to get MHE.

The Haar wavelet coefficients are represented using decimal numbers. The MHE feature is compared with the feature vectors stored in database using Euclidean Distance.

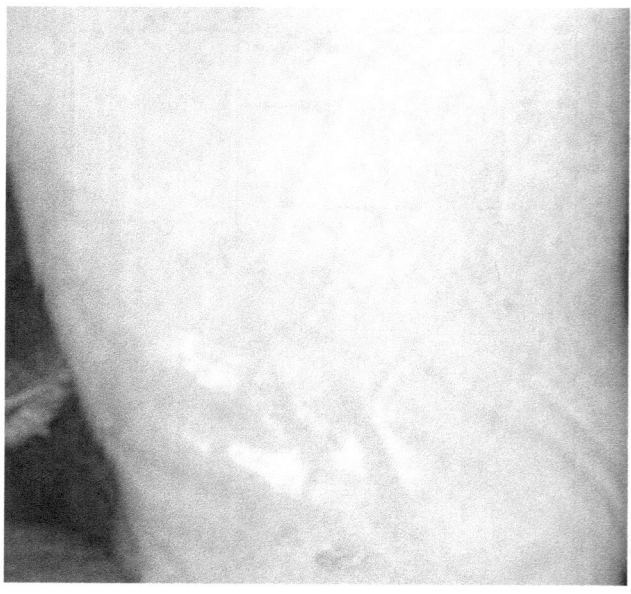

Fig. 9.3 Cropped and grayscale image of foot

The accuracy of the MHE feature and Haar energy feature under different decomposition levels and combinations are compared. Figure 9.3 shows a cropped and gray scale image of foot.

The samples of foot print of different people are cropped and resized. The modified Harr energy of image is obtained by dividing the image into 4 x 4 blocks. The detailed coefficients of every image are then determined. The modified Haar energy for each of the block is calculated as:

$$MHEi, j, k = \sum_{p=1}^{P} \sum_{q=1}^{Q} (C_{p,q})^2 \quad (1)$$

where i is the level of decomposition; j denotes horizontal, vertical or diagonal details; k is the block number from 1 to 16; and P x Q is the size of the block. Figure 9.4 shows 4 x 4 blocks of a foot image.

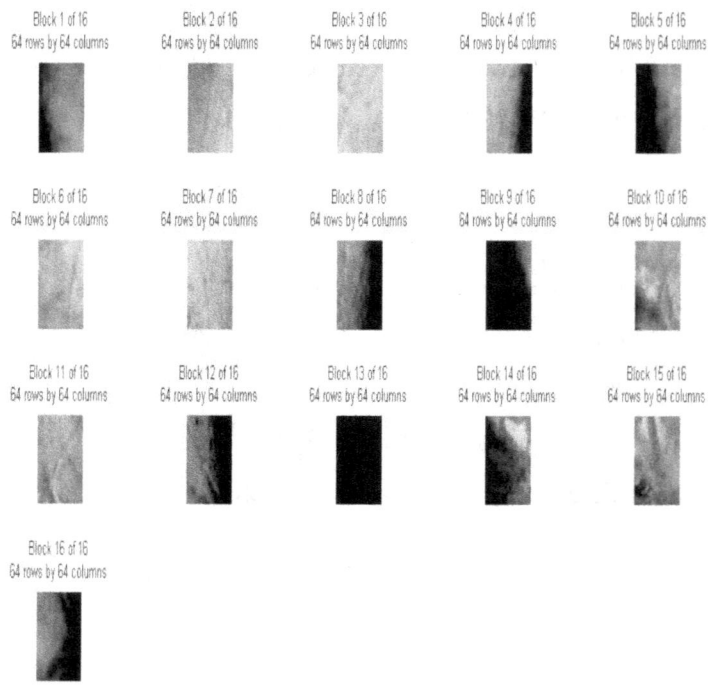

Fig. 9.4 Foot image in 4x4 blocks.

The minimum MHE is selected out of 16 images. Let MHE_1, MHE_2, MHE_3....MHE_{16} be the modified Haar energy values for 16 blocks. Then a modified value is calculated by taking minimum of all the values.

$MHE = \text{Minimum} (MHE_1, MHE_2, \ldots\ldots\ldots MHE_{16})$ (2)

The MHE is compared with the MHE of different persons stored in the database.

CHAPTER 10

CONCLUSION

Biometrics is an important application of digital image processing of biometric modalities. There are several types of biometric security technologies such as face recognition, Ear recognition, Iris recognition, Footprint matching etc. However, there are some prominent challenges in all biometrics dealing with single modality such as reliability, robustness etc. Therefore, multimodal biometrics is recommended which involves more than one modality in the system. AADHAAR card is an example of multimodal biometrics. Multimodal biometrics aims at increasing the reliability of biometric systems. In this book we focused on biometrics modalities, their challenges, concept of multimodal, fusion levels and techniques and at last, implementation of PCA, Eigen images, hamming distance and Modified sequential Haar transformation classifier to four modalities face, ear, iris and foot are shown to get advantage of the Biometrics.

References

[1] A. K. Jain, A. Ross and S. Prabhakar, "An introduction to biometric recognition," *IEEE Transactions on Circuits and Systems for Video Technology*, vol. 14, pp. 4–20, Jan 2003.

[2] A. Ross and A. K. Jain "Multimodal Biometrics: An Overview"*Appeared in Proc. of 12th European Signal Processing Conference (EUSIPCO),* "(Vienna, Austria), September 2004. pp. 1221-1224.

[3] R.Snelick, U.Uludag, A.Mink, M.Indovina, and A.K. Jain,"Large -scale evaluation of multimodal biometric authentication using state-of-the-art systems," *IEEE Transactions on Pattern Analysis and Machine Intelligence*, vol. 27, no. 3, pp. 450 – 455, 2005.

[4] R. Frischholz, and U. Dieckmann, BioID: "A multimodal biometric identification system,," *IEEE Computer,* vol. 33,no.2, pp. 64-68, 2000.

[5] J.Fierrez-Aguilar et al., "A comparative evaluation of fusion strategies for multimodal biometric verification, " *Proc. of the 4 th Int.Con.* J. Kittler, and M. Nixon, Eds., pp. 830 –837,2003.

[6] G.Suganthi and N.Suresh Singh "Ridge Enhanced steganography based on LSB and Arnold Transformation," *ijetcc*, oct 2011, ISSN:2231- 301X,.

[7] S. Barde, "PCA based Multimodal Biometrics using Ear and Face Modalities". International Journal of Information Technology and Computer Science (IJITCS), Vol. 6, No. 5, April 2014, pp: 43-49

[8] R. Singh, M.Vatsa, and A.Noore, "Integrated multilevel image fusion and match score fusion of visible and infrared face images for robust face recognition," Pattern Recognition, vol. 41, pp. 880 –893, 2008.

[9] S. Singh, A. Gyaourova, G. Bebis, and I.Pavlidies, Infrared and visible image fusion for face recognition," *in of SPIE Defense and security symposium,* 2004, pp. 585 –596.

[10] Y.Yao, X.Jing, and H.Wong,"Face and palmprint feature level fusion for single sample biometric recognition," *Nerocomputing,* vol. 70, no. 7-9, pp. 1582 –1586, 2007.

[11] D.R. Kisku, J. K. Singh, M. Tistarelli, and P.Gupta, "Multisensor biometric evidence fusion for person authentication using wavelet decomposition and monotonic decreasing graph," *in Proceedings of 7th International Conference on Adavnaces in Pattern Recognition (ICAPR-2009)*,Kolkata, India, 2009, pp. 205 – 208.

[12] Y.Wang, T.Tan, and A.K.Jain, "Combining Face and Iris Biometrics for Identity Verification," *in proceedings of 4th International Conference on Audio and Video based Biometric Person Authentication* (AVBPA, Guildford, UK),2003, pp 805 – 813.

[13] S. Barde. "Multimodal Biometrics: Most Appropriate For Person Identification" i-manager's Journal on Pattern Recognition, Vol. 4 l No. 3 l September - November 2017, pp:1-8.

[14] A. Ross and A.K. Jain, "Information fusion in biometrics," *Pattern Recognition Letters,* vol. 24, no. 13, pp. 2115 –2125, 2003.

[15] A.Ross and R.Govindarajan, "Feature level fusion using hand and face biome trics," *in Proceedings of SPIE Conference on Biometric Technology for Human Identification,* 2004, pp. 196 –204.

[16] Barde, Snehlata; Zadgaonkar, . "A SPerson Identification Using Face, Ear and Foot Modalities at Rank Level" .i-Manager's Journal on Computer Science; Nagercoil Vol. 2, Iss. 2, (Jun-Aug 2014): 1-8.

[17] S. Prabhakar and A. K. Jain, "Decision level fusion in fingerprint verification," *Pattern Recognit ion*, vol. 35, no. 4, pp. 861 –874, 2002.

[18] P. Xiuqin, X. Xiaona, L. Yong, and C.Youngcun, "Feature fusion of multimodal recognition based on ear and profile face," in *proceedings SPIE* -2008, 2008.

[19] A. Rattani and M. Tistarelli, "Robust multimodal and multiunit feature level fusion of face and iris biometrics," in *international Conference of Biometrics*, Springer, 2009, pp.960 –969.

[20] S. Barde, "Person Identification Using Face, Ear and Foot Modalities." IUP Journal of Computer Sciences. Jan2015, Vol. 9 Issue 1, p32-46. 15p.

[21] Min-Gu Kim1, Hae-Min Moon and Sung Bum Pan. "Framework of Human Identification using Multi Modal Biometrics". *International Journal of Multimedia and Ubiquitous* Engineering Vol. 7, No. 2, April, 2012

[22] S. Barde . "A Certificate of Identification Growth through Multimodal Biometric System" - International Journal of Emerging Trends & Technology, Vol. 2, No. 2, April, 2013

[23] J.Heo, S.Kong, B.Abidi, and M.Abidi, "Fusion of visible and thermal signatures with eyeglass removal for robust face recognition," *in IEEE workshop on Object Tracking and Classification Beyond the visible spectrum in conjunction with (CVPR-2004),* Washington, DC, USA, 2004, pp. 94 –99.

[24] N. Gopal, R.K. Selvakumar, "Multimodal Biometric Identification System –An Overview" *International Journal of Engineering Trends and Technology* (IJETT) Vol. 33 No. 7 March 2016.

www.ingramcontent.com/pod-product-compliance
Lightning Source LLC
Chambersburg PA
CBHW070454220526
45466CB00004B/1821